1935 ... read a good book, you needed
either a lot of money or a library card.
Cheap paperbacks were available, but their
poor production generally mirrored the quality
between the covers. One weekend that year,
Allen Lane, Managing Director of The Bodley Head,
having spent the weekend visiting Agatha Christie,
found himself on a platform at Exeter station trying to
find something to read for his journey back to London.
He was appalled by the quality of the material he had to
choose from. Everything that Allen Lane achieved from that
day until his death in 1970 was based on a passionate belief
in the existence of 'a vast reading public for *intelligent*
books at a low price'. The result of his momentous vision
was the birth not only of Penguin, but of the 'paperback
revolution'. Quality writing became available for the price of
a packet of cigarettes, literature became a mass medium
for the first time, a nation of book-borrowers became a
nation of book-buyers – and the very concept of book
publishing was changed for ever. Those founding
principles – of quality and value, with an overarching
belief in the fundamental importance of reading –
have guided everything the company has
done since 1935. Sir Allen Lane's
pioneering spirit is still very much alive
at Penguin in 2005. Here's to
the next 70 years!

MORE THAN A BUSINESS

'We decided it was time to end the almost customary half-hearted manner in which cheap editions were produced – as though the only people who could possibly want cheap editions must belong to a lower order of intelligence. We, however, believed in the existence in this country of a vast reading public for intelligent books at a low price, and staked everything on it'
Sir Allen Lane, 1902–1970

'The Penguin Books are splendid value for sixpence, so splendid that if other publishers had any sense they would combine against them and suppress them'
George Orwell

'More than a business ... a national cultural asset'
Guardian

'When you look at the whole Penguin achievement you know that it constitutes, in action, one of the more democratic successes of our recent social history'
Richard Hoggart

Christmas at Stalingrad

ANTONY BEEVOR

PENGUIN BOOKS

PENGUIN BOOKS

Published by the Penguin Group
Penguin Books Ltd, 80 Strand, London WC2R ORL, England
Penguin Group (USA) Inc., 375 Hudson Street, New York, New York 10014, USA
Penguin Group (Canada), 10 Alcorn Avenue, Toronto, Ontario, Canada M4V 3B2
(a division of Pearson Penguin Canada Inc.)
Penguin Ireland, 25 St Stephen's Green, Dublin 2, Ireland
(a division of Penguin Books Ltd)
Penguin Group (Australia), 250 Camberwell Road, Camberwell, Victoria 3124,
Australia (a division of Pearson Australia Group Pty Ltd)
Penguin Books India Pvt Ltd, 11 Community Centre,
Panchsheel Park, New Delhi – 110 017, India
Penguin Group (NZ), cnr Airborne and Rosedale Roads, Albany,
Auckland 1310, New Zealand (a division of Pearson New Zealand Ltd)
Penguin Books (South Africa) (Pty) Ltd, 24 Sturdee Avenue,
Rosebank 2196, South Africa

Penguin Books Ltd, Registered Offices: 80 Strand, London WC2R ORL, England

www.penguin.com

Stalingrad first published by Viking 1998
This extract published as a Pocket Penguin 2005

1

Copyright © Antony Beevor and Artemis Cooper, 1998
All rights reserved

The moral right of the author has been asserted

Set in 11/13pt Monotype Dante
Typeset by Palimpsest Book Production Limited
Polmont, Stirlingshire
Printed in England by Clays Ltd, St Ives plc

Part One

Snow began to fall heavily at the end of the first week of December. Drifts filled *balkas*, forcing those who lived in caves excavated from their sides to dig their way out. There was little fuel for any vehicles, and the horses pulling ration carts were so starved that their strength had to be spared on the smallest hills. Chaplain Altmann of the 113th Infantry Division, after hitching a ride on one, recorded: 'I can't remain seated, because the horse is so ill-nourished that he cannot stand the slightest strain.'

Altmann was above all struck by the pathetic youth of soldiers in the regiment he was visiting. Their first question was utterly predictable: 'When are we going to get more to eat?' He also noted that although it was only the second week of December, 'already their wretched bunkers in the middle of this treeless steppe have Christmas decorations'. At battalion headquarters, he received a telephone call warning him of an unChristmas-like duty. 'Tomorrow morning at dawn, execution of a German soldier (nineteen-year-old, self-inflicted wound).'

Although all soldiers suffered badly from hunger, most still had no idea of the size of the supply problem facing the Sixth Army. Hitler, when ordering Paulus to stay in place, had promised that more than one hundred Junkers 52 transport aircraft would be delivering supplies, yet during the air-bridge's first week of operations from 23 November the airlift did not even average thirty flights a day. Twenty-two transport planes were lost through enemy action and crashes on 24 November, and another nine were shot down the following day. Heinkel 111s had to be taken off bombing missions in a desperate attempt to make up the losses. Richthofen rang Jeschonnek three times in an attempt to convince him that they lacked the aircraft to supply the Sixth Army by air. Goering could not be contacted. He had left for Paris.

The airlift did not provide anything like the bare minimum of 300 tons a day promised. Just 350 tons arrived during the course of the whole week. Out of this 350 tons, there were only 14 tons of food for a ration strength by then reduced to 275,000. Three-quarters of the total load consisted of fuel, of which part was for the Luftwaffe's own aircraft based at Pitomnik to protect the transport aircraft from Russian fighters. The Pitomnik-based Messerschmitts, however, were now facing fearsome odds as well as often appalling flying conditions. One captured pilot told his NKVD interrogator how, flying out of Pitomnik as escort, his Me-109 had been cut off and attacked by six Russian fighters.

In the second week up to 6 December, 512 tons (still less than a quarter of the minimum) arrived, delivered by an average of 44 transport aircraft a day. Only 24 tons were food supplies. More and more draught animals had to be slaughtered to make up the shortage. Soldiers saw their rations diminishing rapidly, but they convinced themselves that the situation would not last. They admired the bravery of the Luftwaffe crews and developed a great affection for 'Tante Ju' – the Junkers trimotors flying out wounded comrades and taking their letters home to Germany. 'I'm well and healthy,' they wrote in December, reassuring their families at home. 'Nothing worse can happen,' was another constant refrain. 'Don't be worried for me, I'll soon be home safe and sound.' They still hoped for a Christmas miracle.

Stalin, meanwhile, had been hoping for a second decisive blow, almost immediately after the encirclement of the Sixth Army. Operation Uranus had been seen at the *Stavka* as the first part of a master strategy. The second, and most ambitious phase, would be Operation Saturn. This called for a sudden offensive by the armies of South-West and Voronezh Fronts, smashing through the Italian Eighth Army to advance south to Rostov. The idea was to cut off the rest of Army Group Don and trap the First Panzer and the Seventeenth Armies in the Caucasus.

Even before Sixth Army started to dig in on the steppe between the Don and the Volga, Vasilevsky had been discussing the next stage with the commanders of the South-West and Voronezh Fronts. He submitted his initial project to Stalin on the night of 26 November. The estimated start date for Saturn, allowing for re-deployment and reinforcement, was 10 December. Stalin agreed, and told him to proceed. A more immediate preoccupation, however, had to be addressed first. This was the question of how Manstein would react to save the Sixth Army.

Stalin began to suffer from a characteristic bout of impatience. He wanted everything to happen at once – both Operation Saturn and the rapid destruction of the Sixth Army. He had already given orders for the 2nd Guards Army, the most powerful force in the Red Army, to deploy west of Stalingrad, ready for the attack on Rostov. But as Vasilevsky discovered in the first week of December, even with seven Soviet armies deployed against them, Paulus's divisions were going to be much more difficult to destroy than they had imagined.

On 28 November, Stalin asked Zhukov for an assessment of enemy intentions. Zhukov sent his report the next day. 'The trapped German forces are not likely to try to break out without help from a relief force from the direction of Nizhne-Chirskaya and Kotelnikovo,' he wrote. His predictions proved accurate, but a close study of the situation showed that this was the only practicable choice. After sending his answer to Stalin, Zhukov discussed the situation with Vasilevsky, who had now been told by Stalin to focus his attention entirely on the reduction of the Sixth Army. The two generals privately agreed that they would probably have to postpone Operation Saturn and instead consider an Operation Little Saturn. The plan would be to crash into the rear and left flank of Manstein's Army Group Don. This would bring any drive to relieve Stalingrad to an abrupt halt.

*

Manstein's plan to rescue the Sixth Army – Operation Winter Storm – was developed in full consultation with Führer headquarters (see map). It aimed to break through to the Sixth Army and establish a corridor to keep it supplied and reinforced, so that, according to Hitler's order, it could maintain its 'cornerstone' position on the Volga, 'with regard to operations in 1943'. Manstein, however, who knew that Sixth Army could not survive the winter there, instructed his headquarters to draw up a further plan in the event of Hitler's seeing sense. This would include the subsequent breakout of Sixth Army, in the event of a successful first phase, and its physical reincorporation in Army Group Don. This second plan was given the name Operation Thunderclap.

Winter Storm, as Zhukov had predicted, was originally planned as a two-pronged attack. One thrust would come from the area of Kotelnikovo, well to the south, and around a hundred miles from the Sixth Army. The other would start from the Chir front west of the Don, which was little more than forty miles from the edge of the *Kessel*, but the continuing attacks of Romanenko's 5th Tank Army against the German detachments along the river Chir ruled out that start-line. This left only the LVII Panzer Corps round Kotelnikovo, supported by the rest of Hoth's very mixed Fourth Panzer Army, to relieve Paulus's trapped divisions.

The LVII Panzer Corps, commanded by General Friedrich Kirchner, had been weak at first. It consisted of two Romanian cavalry divisions and the 23rd Panzer

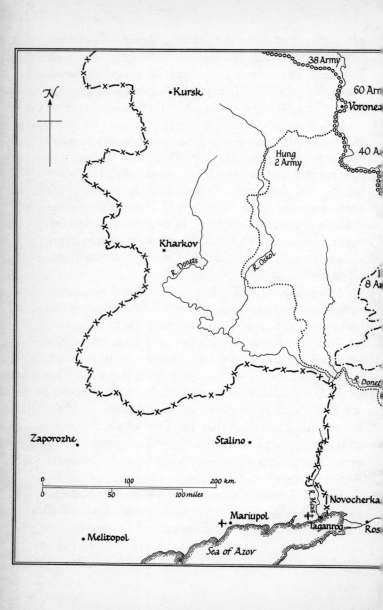

OPERATION WINTER STORM AND OPERATION LITTLE SATURN

○○○○○○	Front line, 12 December 1942
➤	German Operation Winter Storm, 12–23 December 1942
⟪⟪⟪⟪	Soviet Operation Little Saturn, 16–30 December 1942
⟵	Soviet counter–attack on A Gr Hoth, 24–30 December 1942
—·—·—	Front line, 30 December 1942
··········	Front line, 24 January 1943
—x—	Front line, 18 February 1943

5 Sh Army = 5 Shock Army   5 Tk Army = 5 Tank Army
2 Gd Army = 2 Guards Army   LVII Pz C = LVII Panzer Corps

VORONEZH FRONT

Army

1 Gd Army

SOUTH-WEST FRONT

R. Don

DON FRONT

R. Volga

3 Gd Army
Kletskaya

24 Army
66 Army

65 Army

62 Army
Stalingrad

21 Army

• Millerovo

5 Tk Army

Kalach

5 Sh Army

57 Army

2 Gd Army

64 Army

STALINGRAD FRONT

Nizhne-Chirskaya

R. Myshkova

• Morozovsk

Verkhne–Kumsky

R. Aksay

• Tatsinskaya

erevo

51 Army

hakhty

Pakhlebin•

LVII Pz C

R. Don

Kotelnikovo

A Gr Hoth
(4 Pz Army)

28 Army

✝ •Salsk

Division, which mustered no more than thirty service-able tanks. The 6th Panzer Division, arriving from France, was a vastly more powerful formation, but its members hardly received an encouraging impression. The Austrian divisional commander, General Erhard Raus, was summoned to Manstein's royal carriage in Kharkov station on 24 November, where the field marshal briefed him. 'He described the situation in very sombre terms,' recorded Raus. Three days later, when the first trainload of Raus's division steamed into Kotelnikovo station to unload, his troops were greeted by 'a hail of shells' from Soviet batteries. 'As quick as lightning, the panzer grenadiers jumped from their wagons. But already the enemy was attacking the station with their battle-cries of *"Urrah!"'*

Hoth was indeed glad to see the 6th Panzer Division. It had been refitted in Brittany, and was fully up to strength, with 160 long-barrelled Panzer Mark IVs and forty assault guns. The division soon had a chance to try out its new equipment. On 3 December, it became involved in a wild battle with the Soviet 4th Cavalry Corps near the village of Pakhlebin, seven miles north-west of Kotelnikovo. The panzer crews, exhilarated as their tank tracks crunched through the crust of ice in their outflanking armoured charge, cut off the 81st Cavalry Division, inflicting heavy losses. General Raus, pleased with the result, referred to the engagement as 'the Cannae of Pakhlebin'. The arrival of Raus's division confirmed Yeremenko's suspicions that the Germans were about to strike north-eastwards from Kotelnikovo, yet Stalin still refused to transfer reserves to the threatened sector.

Also on 3 December, Hoth produced his proposal for 'Winter Storm', which began: 'Intention: Fourth Panzer Army relieves Sixth Army', but valuable time was lost. The 17th Panzer Division, which was to complete his strike force, had been held back, on the orders of Führer headquarters, as a reserve behind the Italian Eighth Army. In the end it did not join Hoth's force until four days after the operation had begun. Hitler nevertheless insisted that no more time should be wasted. He was also impatient to discover how the new Tiger tank, with its 88-mm gun, would perform. The very first battalion to be formed had been rushed to the *Ostfront* and added to Kirchner's force. On the evening of 10 December, the commanders received the 'Order for the Relief Attack to Stalingrad'.

On 12 December, after a brief artillery bombardment, Hoth's panzers struck north. The German soldiers inside the *Kessel* listened eagerly to the distant sound of fighting. Confidence seemed boundless. Excited rumours ran round the Sixth Army. 'Manstein is coming!' soldiers said to each other, almost like the Easter greeting of the Orthodox Church. For Hitler loyalists, the distant guns were proof once more that the Führer always kept his word.

Hitler, however, had not the slightest intention of allowing the Sixth Army to break out. In his midday conference at the *Wolfsschanze*, he told Zeitzler that it was impossible to retreat from Stalingrad because this would involve sacrificing 'the whole meaning of the campaign' and argued that too much blood had been shed. As Kluge had warned Manstein, he was still obsessed with the events of the previous winter and his order to Army Group Centre to hold fast. 'Once a unit has started to flee,' he lectured the army chief of staff, 'the bonds of law and order quickly disappear in the course of flight.'

The Soviet commanders did not expect Manstein's offensive quite so soon. Yeremenko immediately feared for the 57th Army, which held the south-west corner of the *Kessel*. Vasilevsky was at 51st Army headquarters with Khrushchev on 12 December when the news of the German attack was received in a radio signal. He tried to ring Stalin in Moscow, but could not get through. Not wanting to waste a moment, he contacted General Rokossovsky, the commander of the Don Front, and told him that he wanted to transfer General Rodion Malinovsky's 2nd Guards Army to the command of the Stalingrad Front to block Manstein's offensive. Rokossovsky protested strongly, and to Vasilevsky's dismay when he finally got through to the Kremlin on the telephone that evening, Stalin was angry at what he thought was an attempt to force him into a decision. He refused to give an answer and forced Vasilevsky to spend a very anxious night.

In the meantime, Yeremenko had ordered the 4th Mechanized Corps and the 13th Tank Corps to block the headlong advance of the German armour. The 6th Panzer Division moved forward some thirty miles in the first twenty-four hours, crossing the river Aksay. Finally, after discussions in the Kremlin which lasted into the early hours of the next morning, and more telephone calls with Vasilevsky, Stalin agreed to the transfer of the 2nd Guards Army two days hence.

On the second day of the offensive, 6th Panzer Division reached Verkhne-Kumsky. Rain poured down in what was to prove a brief thaw. On the high ground round this village began what General Raus described as 'a gigantic wrestling-match'. This furious three-day 'revolving battle' became costly. It proved a success locally – Hoth's divisions and the Tiger tanks advanced to the line of the Myshkova, once 17th Panzer Division arrived and Richthofen threw in maximum air support – but events there soon proved irrelevant to the fortunes of the Sixth Army. They were being decided some 125 miles to the north-west.

Stalin quickly realized that Zhukov and Vasilevsky had been right. The most effective way to smash the whole attempt to relieve Paulus's army was by blocking Hoth's advance on the Myshkova, while delivering the decisive blow elsewhere. He agreed to the idea of adapting Operation Saturn. Orders were prepared on the first day of the fighting at Verkhne-Kumsky, instructing the commanders of the Voronezh and South-West Fronts to prepare to launch an amended version, known as Little Saturn. The plan was to smash through the Italian 8th Army into the rear of Army Group Don, rather than strike at Rostov. Their armies were to be ready to attack in three days' time.

Yeremenko was still nervous. With Hoth's Panzer Corps on the line of the Myshkova river, the 6th Panzer Division was less than forty miles from the edge of the *Kessel*, and the 2nd Guards Army, delayed by renewed blizzards, would not be fully in position to counter-attack before 19 December. He expected the Sixth Army's panzer forces to break out from the south-west of the *Kessel* at any moment, but he did not know that Hitler still refused his permission, and that Paulus's seventy remaining tanks had only enough fuel to advance a dozen miles.

Field Marshal von Manstein sent Major Eismann, his intelligence officer, into the *Kessel* by air on 19 December. His mission, Manstein claimed later, was to brief Paulus and Schmidt to prepare the Sixth Army for Operation Thunderclap. Different versions and different interpretations of what was said at this meeting will never be resolved. It is, however, clear that Manstein still avoided taking the responsibility for disobeying Hitler. He would not give Paulus a clear lead, and refused – no doubt, for sound reasons of security – to fly into the *Kessel* to discuss the matter with him face to face. Yet Manstein must have known from the start that Paulus, a firm believer in the chain of command, would never have broken out without a formal order from higher command. Manstein's efforts in his memoirs to absolve himself from any blame for the fate of Sixth Army are curiously exaggerated, as well as unfair on Paulus. It would appear that he suffered from an uneasy conscience, and yet nobody blamed him.

*

On 16 December, just four days into Hoth's offensive, the 1st and 3rd Guards Armies, as well as the Soviet 6th Army further up the Don, attacked south. Slowed by thick, freezing mist, with their tank formations blundering into minefields, the Soviet operation did not get off to a good start. Within two days, however, the Italian Eighth Army had crumbled after some acts of fierce resistance. There was no reserve ready to counterattack, now that the 17th Panzer Division had joined Hoth's operation east of the Don, so the Soviet tank columns broke out southwards into open, snow-covered steppe. The great freeze in the region which began on 16 December did little to slow the brigades of T-34s rampaging in Army Group Don's rear. Railway junctions and stations were captured just after wagons full of equipment had been set ablaze by German support troops before they fled.

The gravest threat to the Germans was the 150-mile advance of Major-General Vasily Mikhailovich Badanov's 24th Tank Corps. On the afternoon of 23 December, it overran Skassirskaya, just to the north of Tatsinskaya, the main Junkers 52 base for Stalingrad. General Fiebig had received an order from Führer headquarters that his aircraft were not to abandon the airfield until it came under artillery fire. Nobody in Hitler's entourage seems to have considered the possibility that an armoured column might arrive at the edge of the field and then open fire.

Fiebig and his officers were furious. One could always recapture an airfield, but if the transport aircraft were lost, then so was the Sixth Army. They had no ground troops to defend 'Tazi', as the Luftwaffe called it. All they could do was to divert seven flak guns to cover the road, and prepare all serviceable aircraft for take-off in the early hours of the morning. There were so many that this did not prove easy. 'Around the runway it looked like chaos,' noted Richthofen's chief of staff, who was present. 'With engines running, one could hardly understand a single word.' To make matters worse, there was a fairly thick mist, cloud was down to 150 feet and light snow was falling.

At 5.20 a.m., the first shells exploded. The bulk of the Soviet tanks had come across country, not up the road. Many pilots, because of the noise and chaos on the airfield, did not at first realize what was happening, even when two Junkers 52s caught fire. Fiebig himself gave the order over the radio, 'Off you go, head for Novocherkassk!' The pilots did not waste time. 'The flight from Tatsinskaya' had started. Considering the earlier confusion, there was impressively little panic. The aircraft took off in a steady stream, despite a mounting rate of casualties. For the Russian T-34s, it was like a shooting range at a fairground. Some of the Soviet tanks fired wildly as they advanced across the snow. One even rammed a Junkers trimotor taxiing into position for take-off. The explosion and fireball consumed them both. Numerous other aircraft crashed into one another on the runway or were destroyed by gunfire. Visibility was becoming worse by the minute, and the remaining aircraft had to negotiate burning wrecks to escape.

Finally at 6.15 a.m., General Fiebig's machine, one of the last to take off, was airborne. Altogether 108 Ju-52 trimotors and 16 Ju-86 trainers were saved, but the loss of 72 aircraft represented roughly 10 per cent of the Luftwaffe's total transport fleet.

Badanov, after this bold raid, found himself cut off for five days, badly mauled and out of ammunition. Stalin was unstinting in his appreciation. The formation was retitled the 2nd Guards Tank Corps, and Badanov was the first to receive the new Order of Suvorov. Red Army propaganda claimed that his tanks had destroyed 431 aircraft in all, but this was a typically wild exaggeration. The important result, however, was that Tatsinskaya was never used for transport missions again. The Luftwaffe had to move even further out to a completely makeshift airfield.

The outcome of Hoth's rescue mission had already been decided. The threat to the left flank of Army Group Don, and the possibility of a breakthrough towards Rostov (apparently confirmed by the interrogation of the chief of staff of the 3rd Guards Army, who was captured on 20 December), forced Manstein to reconsider his whole position. The panzer divisions on the Myshkova were also receiving a heavy battering, with 6th Panzer Division losing 1,100 men in a single day. On the evening of 23 December, Hoth's panzer corps received the order to pull back, without any explanation. 'Right down to the most junior soldier it was absolutely clear', wrote General Raus, 'that this signified defeat at

Stalingrad. Although nobody yet knew the reasons behind the order, officers and men had a strong inkling that something ugly must have happened.'

That same night, Paulus and Manstein discussed the position in a conference conducted via teleprinter. Manstein warned that the 4th Panzer Army had met heavy resistance and that the Italian troops on the northern flank had collapsed. Paulus asked whether he had finally received permission for the Sixth Army to break out. Manstein replied that he still had not obtained agreement from supreme headquarters. He was sparing with the details. If Paulus had been given sufficient information to update his operations map, he would have seen that the Sixth Army was beyond help.

On 16 December, a hard and bitter wind had begun to blow from the north-east. Everything was rimed in frost: telegraph lines, stunted trees, the debris of war. The ground froze so hard that footsteps began to have the ring of walking on metal. As night fell, following a vivid red sunset, the white landscape briefly turned an arctic blue. The Russian defenders of Stalingrad welcomed the cold as natural and healthy. 'Yesterday and today winter really started here,' a soldier wrote to his wife. 'Good frosts. I live very well, but no letters from you.'

Nobody was happier than the members of Chuikov's 62nd Army in Stalingrad itself, after five weeks of listening to the terrible grinding of the ice floes on the virtually unnavigable Volga, and subsisting off the emergency reserve of twelve tons of chocolate and tiny supply drops by U-2 biplanes. The river finally froze solid on the night of 16 December, when a mass of ice floes crushed and stuck firm. First a footway over the ice was made with planks. Then motor highways were constructed using branches and water poured over them, which froze and bound the surface. In the course of the next seven weeks, tracked vehicles, 18,000 lorries and 17,000 other vehicles crossed over. Any wounded could now be driven straight across the ice to the field hospital. Guns were later trundled across to the west bank, including a 122-mm howitzer which was needed to break the deadlock in the Red October works. On minimum elevation, it was used at short range to blast the main office building, which the Germans had turned into a fortress.

Most fortunate of all for the 62nd Army, the short-age of shells for the German artillery meant that the constant shelling of Volga crossing points was no longer possible. The bank itself often offered a peace-ful scene. It resembled an early frontier mining settle-ment, with makeshift huts and tarpaulin shelters over holes in the bank. As men split logs, or sawed wood, a regimental postman walked past in the frozen sunshine to headquarters with his leather mailbag, hoping for a mug of hot tea from the copper samovar. Others went by bearing thermos containers with hot food for the troops in forward positions. Soldiers could now walk back in batches over the ice to steam baths set up on the east side of the river, to return clean and deloused the next night.

On 19 December General Chuikov crossed to the east

bank of the Volga for the first time since changing his headquarters in October. He crossed the ice on foot, and when he reached the far side, he apparently turned to gaze at the ruins which his army had held. Chuikov had come over for a party given by the commander of NKVD troops, Major-General Rogatin, in honour of the twenty-fourth anniversary of the founding of the Special Department of the Cheka. Chuikov on his return, when very drunk, fell through a hole in the ice, and had to be fished out of the freezing water. The commander of the 62nd Army nearly met an ignominious and anti-climactic end.

While the Russians welcomed the low temperatures, the doctors in Paulus's army dreaded them, for several reasons. The resilience of their patients, both the sick and the wounded, declined. Frost in an open wound could rapidly prove lethal. The hardness of the ground when shells, *Katyusha* rockets and mortar bombs exploded, seemed to be the only explanation for the great increase in stomach wounds with which they were faced. And from the middle of December there was 'a steadily increasing number of serious frostbite cases'. The feet were not just swollen and purple – a degree treated with ointment, a bandage and return to duty – but black and potentially gangrenous, often requiring rapid amputation.

As early as the second week of December, doctors had started to notice a more disturbing phenomenon. An increasing number of soldiers died suddenly 'without having received a wound or suffering from a diagnosable sickness'. Rations were indeed severely reduced, but for doctors, it still appeared to be far too early for cases of death by starvation. 'The suspected causes', wrote the pathologist entrusted with the inquiry, 'included exposure, "exhaustion" [none of the approximately 600 doctors in the *Kessel* ventured to mention starvation] and above all a hitherto unidentified disease.'

On 15 December, Dr Girgensohn, the Sixth Army pathologist then working in the hospital next to Tatsinskaya airfield, received the order to fly into the *Kessel* next day. 'Unfortunately we don't have a spare parachute for you,' the pilot told him when he reported next morning at dawn, but they were forced to turn back. Finally, on 17 December, they reached the *Kessel*. The pilot told him they were over Pitomnik, and Girgensohn, peering through the small window, saw 'in the white blanket of snow a brown cratered landscape'.

Girgensohn found General Doctor Renoldi, the chief medical officer, in a railway carriage dug into the ground on the edge of the airfield. Renoldi pretended to know nothing about Girgensohn's mission, because Dr Seggel, a specialist in internal medicine at Leipzig University, had requested his presence, and Renoldi, at that stage, considered the issue exaggerated.* From Pitomnik, Girgensohn was taken to the army field hospital next

---

* General Doctor Renoldi took more interest later. From his railway carriage, he rather chillingly described the collapse of soldiers' health in the *Kessel* as 'a large-scale experiment into the effects of hunger'.

to Gumrak station and also close to Paulus's headquarters. His base was a wood-lined bunker, dug into the steep side of a *balka*. This accommodation was indeed 'luxurious', since it contained an iron stove and two double bunk beds with, to his astonishment, clean sheets. It was a great contrast to the nearby accommodation for the wounded, which largely consisted of unheated tents in temperatures down to minus twenty.

Girgensohn had preliminary discussions with divisional medical officers, then travelled round the *Kessel*, carrying out post-mortems on the corpses of soldiers who had died from no obvious causes. (Such was the shortage of wood in this treeless waste that a fork or crossroads along the snowbound route was marked by the leg from a slaughtered horse stuck upright in a mound of snow. The relevant tactical sign and directional arrow were attached to the top of this gruesome signpost.) The autopsies had to be carried out in a variety of inconvenient places: tents, earth bunkers, peasant huts, even in railway wagons. The extreme cold had maintained the cadavers in good condition, but most were frozen solid. Thawing them out proved very difficult with the shortage of available fuel. An orderly had to spend the night turning the corpses stacked around a small cast-iron oven. On one occasion, he fell asleep, and the result was 'a corpse frozen on one side and seared on the other'.

The cold was so bad that it was both difficult and painful for Girgensohn to pull on his rubber gloves. Each evening, he typed up the results by candlelight. In spite of such difficulties, which included Soviet air attacks and artillery bombardments, Girgensohn managed to perform fifty autopsies by the end of the month. In exactly half of this sample, he found clear signs of death by starvation: atrophy of the heart and liver, a complete absence of fatty tissue, a severe shrinkage of muscle.

In an attempt to compensate for the low-calorie diet of bread and '*Wasserzuppe*' with a few tiny bits of horsemeat, Army Group Don flew in small tins of meat paste with a high fat content, but this proved counter-productive. Quite often, when a sergeant was making his rounds of the sentry positions and a soldier said, 'I'm fine, I'll now have something to eat,' and then consumed some of the high-fat meat paste, the man was dead by the time the sergeant made his next round. Death from starvation, Girgensohn observed, was '*undramatisch*'.

The highest proportion of cases of death by starvation occurred in the 113th Infantry Division. Here at least, Girgensohn discovered a clear explanation. The quartermaster of the division had cut rations before the encirclement to hoard them as a precaution against insufficient supplies during the autumn rains. As a result, the men were already undernourished by the second half of November. Then, after several divisions had lost all their supplies during the retreat, Sixth Army headquarters centralized all remaining supplies to share them out equally. Thus the quartermaster's prudence backfired badly against his division.

Girgensohn, who spent seven years in Russian labour camps after the surrender, never lost his interest in the

subject. He has always vigorously disputed any sugges-
tion of 'stress illness', both as a condition in itself, and
as an explanation for many of the unexplained deaths,
even though recent research, which has shown that rats
deprived of sleep for three weeks will die, suggests that
humans deprived of sleep burn out rapidly. The pattern
of Russian night attacks and constant activity to allow
no rest undoubtedly had a contributory effect, as he
acknowledges. But his explanation, after all these years,
is more complex. He became convinced that the combin-
ation of exhaustion, stress and cold gravely upset the
metabolism of most soldiers. This meant that even if
they received the equivalent of, say, 500 calories a day,
their bodies absorbed only a fraction. Thus, one could
say that Soviet tactics, combined with the weather
conditions and food shortages, produced, or at least
contributed to, an accelerated process of starvation.

Severe malnutrition also reduced a patient's ability to
survive infectious diseases, such as hepatitis and dysen-
tery in the earlier period of the encirclement, and more
serious diseases right at the end, particularly typhoid
and typhus. Out in the steppe there was no water for
washing bodies, let alone clothes, simply because there
was not enough fuel to melt snow and ice. 'There's little
new here,' wrote a panzer grenadier lieutenant in the
29th Motorized Infantry Division. 'Top of the list is the
fact that every day we become more infested with lice.
Lice are like the Russians. You kill one, ten new ones
appear in its place.' Lice would be the carriers for the
epidemics which decimated the survivors of Stalingrad.

The immediate concerns of medical staff, however, still focused on weakness from lack of food. 'Slowly, our brave fighters are starting to become decrepit,' wrote an assistant doctor. He went on to describe an amputation at the thigh which he performed by torchlight in a dugout without any form of anaesthetic. 'One is apathetic towards everything and can only think about food.'

The need of German soldiers for hope was mixed with a hatred for the Bolshevik enemy and a longing for revenge. In a state of what was called 'Kesselfever', they dreamed of an SS Panzer Corps smashing through the encircling Russian armies to rescue them, thus turning the tables in a great, unexpected victory. They tended to be the ones who still listened to Goebbels's speeches. Many kept up their spirits by singing the Sixth Army's song, *Das Wolgalied*, to the tune by Franz Lehár: 'There stands a soldier on the Volga shore, keeping watch there for his Fatherland'.

The operational propaganda department at Don Front headquarters, using its German Communist assistants, decided to exploit the *Landser*'s fondness for songs. They broadcast from their loudspeaker vans an old favourite, which in present circumstances had a cruel twist: 'In the homeland, in the homeland, there awaits a warm reunion!' The German Communists under NKVD supervision consisted of Walter Ulbricht (later the East German president), the poet Erich Weinart, the writer Willi Bredel and a handful of German prisoners

– four officers and a soldier – who had been recruited to the anti-Nazi cause. They taught 'criers', who were Red Army men chosen to crawl forward to dead ground in front of German lines and shout slogans and items of news through megaphones. Few of them knew any German, and most were killed.

The main activity of the propaganda detachment was to prepare 20- to 30-minute programmes on a gramophone record, with music, poems, songs and propaganda (especially the news of the breakthrough on the Italian Army's front). The programme was then played on a wind-up gramophone, and broadcast by the loudspeakers, either mounted on the van, or sometimes pushed forwards on sledges with a wire running back. Most propaganda broadcasts of this sort immediately attracted German mortar fire, on the order of officers afraid that their men might listen. But during December, the response became weaker owing to the shortage of munitions.

Different sound tricks were adopted, such as 'the monotonous ticking of a clock' followed by the claim that one German died every seven seconds on the Eastern Front. The 'crackling sound of the propaganda voice' then intoned: 'Stalingrad, mass grave of Hitler's army!' and the deathly tango dance music would start up again across the empty frozen steppe. As an extra sonic twist, the heart-stopping shriek of a real *Katyusha* rocket would sometimes follow from a 'Stalin organ' launcher.

Russian leaflets had greatly improved, now that they

were written by Germans. Prisoner interrogations by the 7th Department confirmed that 'the ones with the most effect are those which talk about home, wives, family and children'. 'Soldiers eagerly read Russian leaflets even though they don't believe them,' admitted one German prisoner. Some 'cried when they saw a leaflet representing the corpse of a German soldier and an infant crying over it. On the other side were simple verses by the writer Erich Weinart.' The prisoner had no idea that Weinart, who had specially written the poem, 'Think of Your Child!', was very close by, attached to Don Front headquarters.

Perhaps the most effective piece of propaganda was to persuade German soldiers that they would not be shot on capture. Many of their officers had relied on the argument that surrender was out of the question because the Russians would kill them. One leaflet ended with a declaration by Stalin which began to convince even junior commanders that Soviet policy had changed: '"If German soldiers and officers give themselves up, the Red Army must take them prisoner and spare their lives." (From Order No. 55 by the People's Commissar for Defence, J. Stalin.)'

The first encirclement of a large German army, trapped far from home, ordered to stay put and finally abandoned to its fate, has naturally created an intense debate over the years. Many German participants and historians have blamed Paulus for not having disobeyed orders, and broken out. Yet if anybody was in a position to give

25

Paulus, who was deprived of vital information, a lead in the matter, it should have been his immediate superior, Field Marshal von Manstein.

'Can one serve two masters?' Strecker noted when Hitler rejected Operation Thunderclap, the breakout plan to follow Operation Winter Storm. But the German Army only had a single master. The servile record since 1933 of most senior officers had left it both dishonoured and politically impotent. In fact, the disaster and humiliation of Stalingrad were the price which the army had to pay for its hubristic years of privilege and prestige under the National Socialist umbrella. There was no choice of master, short of joining the group round Henning von Tresckow and Stauffenberg.

Much time has been spent debating whether a breakout was feasible in the second half of December, yet even panzer commanders acknowledged that 'the chances of a successful breakout diminished with every week'. The infantry had even fewer illusions. 'We survivors', a corporal wrote home, 'can hardly keep going owing to hunger and weakness.' Dr Alois Beck, quite rightly, disputed the 'legend' that 'a breakout would have succeeded'. The Russians would have shot the 'half-frozen soldiers down like hares', because the men in their weakened state could not have waded through over a foot of snow, with its crust of ice on the surface, carrying weapons and ammunition. 'Every step was exhausting,' observed a staff officer from Sixth Army headquarters. 'It would have been like the Berezina.'

The whole 'Breakout or Defence' debate is thus a purely academic diversion from the real issues. In fact one suspects that the formidably intelligent Manstein recognized this at the time. He made a great play of sending Major Eismann, his intelligence officer, into the *Kessel* on 19 December to prepare the Sixth Army for Operation Thunderclap. Yet Manstein knew by then that Hitler, who had again reaffirmed his determination not to move from the Volga, would never change his mind.

In any case, Manstein must have realized by then that the relief attempt was doomed. Hoth's panzer divisions were being fought to a standstill on the Myshkova, with heavy casualties, even before the bulk of Malinovsky's 2nd Guards Army had deployed. And Manstein, who had kept himself well informed of developments within the *Kessel* and the state of the troops, must have realized that Paulus's men could never have walked, let alone fought, for between forty and sixty miles through the blizzards and deep frosts. The Sixth Army, with fewer than seventy under-supplied tanks, stood no chance of breaking through the 57th Army. Most important of all, Manstein knew by 19 December that Operation Little Saturn, with three Soviet armies breaking through into his rear, was changing the whole position irrevocably.

Quite simply, Manstein sensed that, in the sight of history and the German Army, he had to be seen to make every effort, even if he believed, quite correctly, that the Sixth Army's only chance of saving itself had expired almost a month earlier. His apparently uneasy conscience after the event must have been due to the fact that, with Hitler's refusal to withdraw from the Caucasus, he had needed the Sixth Army to tie down the seven Soviet armies surrounding it. If Paulus had attempted a break-out so few of his men would have survived, and in such a pitiable condition, that they would have been of no use to him in the moment of crisis.

Part Two

The argument about breaking out of the *Kessel* in the second half of December also overlooked one curiously important psychological factor. Christmas was coming. No formation in the Wehrmacht was more preoccupied with the subject than the beleaguered Sixth Army. The quite extraordinary efforts devoted to its observance in bunkers below the steppe hardly indicated an impatience to break out. Lethargy from malnutrition combined with escapist daydreaming no doubt played a part, and probably so did the 'Fortress' mentality which Hitler helped to cultivate. But none of these entirely explain the almost obsessive emotional focus which the prospect of Christmas held for those trapped so far from home.

Preparations began well before Hoth's panzer divisions advanced north to the Myshkova river, and never seem to have slackened, even when soldiers became excited by the sound of approaching gunfire. From quite early in the month, men started to put aside tiny amounts of food, not in preparation for a breakout across the snow, but for a Christmas feast or for gifts. A unit in 297th Infantry Division slaughtered a packhorse early so as to make 'horse sausage' as Christmas presents. Advent crowns were fashioned from tawny steppe grass instead of evergreen, and little Christmas trees were carved out of wood in desperate attempts to make it 'just like at home'.

The sentimentality was by no means restricted to soldiers. General Edler von Daniels decorated his newly dug bunker with a Christmas tree and underneath a cradle with a snapshot of his 'Kesselbaby', born soon after their encirclement. He wrote to his young wife describing his plans to celebrate Christmas Eve 'in the German way, although in far-off Russia'. The military group had clearly become the surrogate family. 'Each man sought to bring a little joy to another,' he wrote after visiting his men in their bunkers. 'It was really uplifting to experience this true comradeship of the front line.' One festive banner proclaimed 'Comradeship through Blood and Iron', which, however appropriate to the circumstances, rather missed the message of Christmas.

One person who certainly did not miss the message was Kurt Reuber, the doctor in the 16th Panzer Division. The thirty-six-year-old Reuber, a theologian and friend of Albert Schweitzer, was also a gifted amateur artist. He converted his bunker in the steppe north-west of Stalingrad into a studio and began to draw on the back of a captured Russian map – the only large piece of paper to be found. This work, which today hangs in the Kaiser Wilhelm memorial church in Berlin, is the 'Fortress Madonna', an embracing, protective, almost womb-like mother and child, joined with the words of St John the Evangelist: 'Light, Life, Love'. When the drawing was finished, Reuber pinned it up in the bunker.

Everyone who entered, halted and stared. Many began to cry. To Reuber's slight embarrassment – no artist could have been more modest about his own gifts – his bunker became something of a shrine.

There can be little doubt about the genuine and spontaneous generosity of that Christmas. A lieutenant gave out the last of his cigarettes, writing paper and bread as presents for his men. 'I myself had nothing,' he wrote home, 'and yet it was one of my most beautiful Christmases and I will never forget it.' As well as giving their cigarette ration, men even gave their bread, which they sorely needed. Others laboriously carved equipment racks for each other.

On Christmas Eve, Reuber's pianist battalion commander gave his last bottle of sparkling wine to the soldiers in the sickbay, but just after all the mugs were filled, four bombs exploded outside. Everyone flung themselves to the floor, spilling all the Sekt. The medical officer grabbed his first-aid bag and ran from the bunker to see to the casualties – one killed and three wounded. The dead man had been singing the Christmas carol '*O du fröhliche*'. The incident, not surprisingly, put an end to their celebrations. In any case, both the 16th Panzer and the 60th Motorized Infantry Division soon found themselves under full attack in the early hours of Christmas morning.

The traditional, and favourite, song that night was '*Stille Nacht, heilige Nacht*', which soldiers sang 'with husky voices' in bunkers by the light of hoarded candle stubs. There were many stifled sobs as men thought of their families at home. General Strecker was clearly moved when he made a tour of front-line positions. 'It is a "Stille Nacht" amid the turmoil of war . . . A Christmas that shows the true brotherhood of soldiers.' Visits by senior officers were also appreciated for their accompanying benefits. An NCO in a panzer division recorded that 'the divisional commander gave us a swig from his bottle and a bar of chocolate'.

In positions which were not attacked, men crowded into a bunker which had a wireless to hear 'the Christmas broadcast of Grossdeutsche Rundfunk'. To their astonishment, they heard a voice announce: 'This is Stalingrad!', answered by a choir singing *Stille Nacht, heilige Nacht*, supposedly on the Volga front. Some men accepted the deception as necessary in the circumstances, others were deeply angered. They felt it was tricking their families and the German people as a whole. Goebbels had already proclaimed that this should be a 'German Christmas', a definition intended to convey notions of duty and austerity, and perhaps already a way of preparing the nation for news of the tragedy of Stalingrad.

At seven o'clock on Christmas morning, the Sixth Army war diary recorded: 'No supply flights arrived in the last forty-eight hours [a slight exaggeration]. Supplies and fuel coming to an end.' Later that day, Paulus sent a warning signal to Army Group Don to be passed back to General Zeitzler. 'If we do not receive increased rates of supplies in the next few days, we must expect a greatly increased death rate through exhaustion.'

Although they realized that the snowstorms of the previous day must have hindered flying, they had not been informed that Badanov's tanks had stormed on to Tatsinskaya airfield the previous morning. Manstein's headquarters did not even pass on the news that the Soviet counter-attack with four armies against Hoth's panzer divisions on the Myshkova river had been launched. When 108 tons of supplies finally arrived on 26 December, Sixth Army headquarters discovered that they had been sent ten tons of sweets for Christmas, but no fuel.

Most men, when they had the opportunity, sat apart to write a Christmas letter home in which they expressed their longing. 'In our hearts we all keep hoping', wrote a doctor with the 44th Infantry Division, 'that everything will change.' He spoke for many, but the better-informed commander-in-chief of the Sixth Army was not among them. 'Christmas naturally was not very joyful,' Paulus wrote to his wife a few days later. 'At such moments, festivities are better avoided . . . One should not, I believe, expect too much from luck.'

Not surprisingly, the contrast between German and Russian letters home during the Christmas period becomes even more marked than usual. While German letters tended to be sentimental, aching for home and family, the Russian letters that have survived clearly reveal an inexorable logic that the Motherland took priority. 'Darling!' wrote a soldier to his wife on Christmas Eve. 'We are pushing the serpents back to where they came from. Our successful advance brings our next meeting closer.' 'Hello Mariya,' wrote a soldier called Kolya. 'I've been fighting here for three months defending our beautiful [deleted by censor]. We have started pressing the enemy strongly. Now we have encircled the Germans. Every week a few thousand are taken prisoner and several thousand are destroyed on the field of battle. There are just the most stubborn SS soldiers left. They have fortified themselves in bunkers and shoot from them. And now I'm going to blow up one of those bunkers. Goodbye. Kolya.'

The temperature on Christmas Day fell to minus twenty-five degrees. The water in shell holes, however deep, was frozen solid. Flurries of snow hid much of the squalor in the *balkas*. Chaplains held field mass or communion in the snow to the sound of tarpaulins and tent canvas flapping and cracking in the wind, with half circles of men round a makeshift altar. In some cases, spiritual comfort and ideological justification became confused, as when Christian Germany was contrasted with godless Russia.

Even within the *Kessel*, Christmas did not prove entirely a season of goodwill. Dr Renoldi, the Sixth Army's surgeon-general, forbade the evacuation by air of frost-bite casualties, on the grounds that their injuries might have been self-inflicted to avoid combat. And worst of all, virtually no food, apart from some rotting corn from the Stalingrad grain elevator, had been given to the 3,500 Russian prisoners of war in the camps at Voroponovo and Gumrak, because they did not feature on any ration strength. This partly bureaucratic atrocity led to a death rate of twenty a day by Christmas, and it soon escalated dramatically. The quartermaster responsible for feeding them claimed that typhus was the cause, but when an officer from Sixth Army headquarters asked whether there had been deaths from undernourishment, he was evasive. 'After reflecting for a moment, he denied it,' wrote the officer. 'I knew what he meant. Among our troops one was beginning to see similar things.' But linking their fate with that of German soldiers was a worse evasion. The inmates had no choice – they could not surrender. Even when desperate prisoners began to resort to cannibalism, nothing was done to improve their conditions, because that meant 'taking food from German soldiers'.

Christmas night was 'a beautiful starry night' and the temperature fell even further. Fighting, however, continued the next morning in the north-eastern sector of the *Kessel* defended by 16th Panzer Division and 60th Motorized Infantry Division. 'Thus a dozen of our units', reported the latter's divisional chaplain, 'were sent out to counter-attack in icy winds and thirty-five degrees of frost.' The two divisions, despite the terrible conditions and shortages of ammunition, managed to destroy some seventy tanks.

On that same morning of 26 December, Paulus sent another signal to Manstein, which began: 'Bloody losses, cold and insufficient supplies have reduced fighting strength of divisions severely.' He warned that if the Russians brought back their forces fighting Hoth's divisions, and redeployed them against the Sixth Army, 'it would not be possible to withstand them for long'.

An unexpected opportunity then arose. General Hube, the commander of XIV Panzer Corps, received an order to fly out of the *Kessel* on 28 December to Manstein's headquarters at Novocherkassk. An aircraft would take him on to East Prussia to receive the Swords to his Knight's Cross with Oak Leaves from the Führer in person. Paulus told Schmidt to give him 'all the necessary documents' on all matters from fuel levels to shortages of medical equipment. The hopes of generals and staff officers leaped at the news of his visit to Rastenburg. Hube, the blunt, one-armed veteran, was one of the few generals that the Führer respected. They still could not believe 'that Hitler would abandon the Sixth Army'.

Hitler had no doubt convinced himself that he was doing everything to save the Sixth Army, but his grasp of reality had not improved. That day his headquarters signalled to Army Group Don, promising that in spite of the bad transport situation, it would be reinforced with '372 tanks and assault guns'. Manstein knew that this was wishful thinking.

In the city of Stalingrad, meanwhile, the remnants of Seydlitz's divisions were on the defensive. They had to conserve ammunition to repel attacks. They sheltered deep in cellars and bunkers, for warmth as well as safety from the Soviet artillery. 'There they sit like hairy savages in stone-age caves,' wrote Grossman, 'devouring horseflesh in smoke and gloom, amidst the ruins of a beautiful city that they have destroyed.'

The phrase 'strong enemy storm troop activity'

appeared frequently in the Sixth Army war diary. Hans Urban, a twenty-eight-year-old police-station sergeant from Darmstadt, serving with the Hessian 389th Infantry Division, later provided a detailed report of this fighting in northern Stalingrad at the end of December.

The enemy used to attack at dawn and at dusk, after a heavy artillery and mortar preparation. If they captured two or three bunkers from us, we would try to get them back later. On 30 December, after many of these attacks, I was ordered to take my rapid-fire group forward. My nine men with their machine-guns were able to hold off the next attack by about 300 men from Spartakovka. The twenty infantrymen left on this sector were so exhausted from all the attacks that they could not offer much help. Most were ready to abandon their positions. I had with my two machine-guns no field of fire. The enemy were able to make use of the terrain and the ruins. We had to let the Russians get to within twenty yards before opening rapid fire. At least twenty-two were left dead in front of our positions. The surviving Russians tried to flush us out with grenades. The Russians attacked again on the same sector at daybreak on New Year's morning with three companies. It's hard to make an accurate estimate because they were shooting from holes in the ground, from behind collapsed walls or piles of rubble. We got them in a cross-fire from the two machine-guns, and they suffered heavy casualties. A mortar-man was hit, and although I'd never trained with the weapon, we were able to use their own ammunition against them. After it was over, we were so weak and exhausted and there were so many dead lying around in the open frozen stiff, that we could not even bury our own comrades.

Paulus, in contrast to his strongly pessimistic signals to Army Group Don and the letter to his wife, signed a stirring New Year message to the Sixth Army: 'Our will for victory is unbroken and the New Year will certainly bring our release! When this will be, I cannot yet say. The Führer has, however, never gone back on his word, and this time will be no different.'

Thanks to Hitler's insistence on time zones, the Russian New Year arrived two hours earlier than the German. General Edler von Daniels's card game of 'Doppelknopf' was interrupted at ten o'clock by 'a powerful firework display', as the Soviet besiegers fired in their 'New Year greeting'.

Daniels appears to have been in a good mood at this time. He had just been promoted to Lieutenant-General and awarded the Knight's Cross. Then, as a New Year's present from Paulus, he unexpectedly received a bottle of Veuve-Cliquot 'Schampus'. Several of the Stalingrad generals still seemed to be almost more preoccupied with decorations and promotions than with the fate of the Sixth Army.

When German midnight arrived, only star shells were fired. High-explosive rounds could not be wasted. The very last bottles were opened in the *Kessel* for the toast: '*Prosit Neujahr!*' Soviet divisions, on the other hand, suffered few restrictions on ammunition and alcohol.

'Celebrating the New Year was good,' wrote Viktor Barsov, in the marine infantry. 'I drank 250 grams of vodka that night. The food wasn't bad. In the morning to avoid a headache I drank 200 grams more.'

German soldiers tried to make light of their misfortunes, with the idea that everything would change for the better with the passing of the old year. 'Dear Parents, I'm all right,' wrote one soldier. 'Unfortunately, I again have to go on sentry tonight. I hope that in this New Year of 1943, I won't have to survive as many disappointments as in 1942.'

An almost obsessive optimism was produced by Hitler's New Year message to Paulus and the Sixth Army. Only the more sceptical spotted that the text did not constitute a firm guarantee. 'In the name of the whole German people, I send you and your valiant army the heartiest good wishes for the New Year. The hardness of your perilous position is known to me. The heroic stand of your troops has my highest respect. You and your soldiers, however, should enter the New Year with the unshakeable confidence that I and the whole German Wehrmacht will do everything in our power to relieve the defenders of Stalingrad and that with your staunchness will come the most glorious feat in the history of German arms. Adolf Hitler.'

'*Mein Führer!*' Paulus replied immediately. 'Your confident words on the New Year were greeted here with great enthusiasm. We will justify your trust. You can be certain that we – from the oldest general to the youngest grenadier – will hold out, inspired with a fanatical will, and contribute our share to final victory. Paulus.' New Year letters from many soldiers in the *Kessel* reflected a new mood of determination. 'We're not letting our spirits sink, instead we believe in the word of the Führer,' wrote a captain. 'We are maintaining a firm trust in the Führer, unshakeable until final victory,' wrote an NCO. 'The Führer knows our worries and needs,' wrote a soldier, 'he will always – and I'm certain of this – try to help us as quickly as possible.' Even a sceptical general like Strecker seems to have been affected. 'New hope arises,' he wrote, 'and there is some optimism about the present and immediate future.'

Paulus, on the other hand, was concerned at this time by the growing success of Soviet propaganda. The 7th Department at Don Front headquarters in charge of 'operational propaganda' had followed up their identification of 44th Infantry Division and General Edler von Daniels's 376th Infantry Division as the formations on which they should concentrate their efforts

Early on the morning of 3 January, Paulus went to the Austrian 44th Infantry Division, 'following radio broadcasts by prisoners from the 44th Infantry Division'. They had spoken on the shortages of food and ammunition and about the heavy casualties. 'The commander-in-chief', stated the Sixth Army report, 'wanted warnings to be given about the consequences of partaking in such broadcasts. Any soldiers who did so should realize that their names would be known, and they would face court martial.' During Paulus's meeting with General Deboi, the divisional commander, there was yet another 'heavy attack with tanks'.

The very next morning, Paulus visited the Romanian commander in the 'Fortress area', whose soldiers had suffered serious frostbite casualties owing to clothing shortages, 'above all boots, trousers and socks'. The rising number of desertions prompted Paulus to conclude that: 'Counter-propaganda is necessary against Russian leaflets printed in Romanian.'

Battalions and companies were so weak that they had become meaningless designations. Out of over 150,000 soldiers left in the *Kessel*, less than one in five were front-line troops. Many companies were down to a dozen men fit for duty. Fragments of units were therefore increasingly amalgamated into battle groups. The surviving panzer grenadiers of Sergeant-Major Wallrawe's company found themselves mixed 'with Luftwaffe companies and Cossack platoons' and sent to defend a position near Karpovka. It was an unfortunate spot to be sent to. A glance at the map indicated that the 'nose' which formed the south-western extremity of the *Kessel* would be the Russians' first objective when they decided to finish off the Sixth Army.

There were a few days of comparatively mild, wet weather at the very start of the year. Russian soldiers hated the thaw. 'I don't like the weather in Stalingrad', wrote Barsov in the marine infantry. 'It changes often and this makes the rifles go rusty. When it becomes warmer, the snow starts to fall. Everything becomes moist. *Valenki* [felt snow-boots] become soaking wet and we don't get much chance to dry things.' He and his comrades were, no doubt, happier on 5 January, when the temperature dropped to minus thirty-five degrees.

Soviet forces adopted a deliberate tactic to exploit their superiority in winter equipment. 'The Russians began with probing attacks', wrote a Luftwaffe liaison officer. 'If they breached the line, none of our men were in a position to dig new fire trenches. The men were physically too weak owing to lack of food, and the ground was frozen rock-hard.' Stranded on the open steppe, even more would die. On 6 January, Paulus signalled to General Zeitzler: 'Army starving and frozen, have no ammunition and cannot move tanks any more.' The same day, Hitler awarded General Schmidt the Knight's Cross of the Iron Cross.

Now that the fate of the Sixth Army was certain, Soviet journalists were brought to Don Front headquarters at Zavarykino. A delegation of Soviet writers came down from the capital to visit the 173rd Rifle Division, which had been raised from the Kievsky district of Moscow, and contained many intellectuals. 'From the command post of 65th Army, writers Aleksandr Korneychuk and Wanda Vasilevskaya' watched the division attack the Kazachy Kurgan, a Tartar burial mound on the north-west of the *Kessel*.

Even before Hoth's rescue attempt had been crushed on the Myshkova river, Stalin was harrying his generals to produce plans for the annihilation of the Sixth Army. On the morning of 19 December, he had telephoned

Voronov, the *Stavka* representative overseeing Operation Little Saturn, and told him to move to Don Front headquarters. Voronov installed himself close to Rokossovsky's 'residenz', spread across the adjoining villages of Zavarykino and Medvedevo, where the accommodation for each general, or department, consisted of a 'five-walled' peasant *izba*, a log cabin with a dividing wall down the middle. American Willis staff cars, with Soviet markings, lurched in and out of the frozen ruts, taking generals off on tours of inspection to galvanize subordinate commanders in their efforts.

Voronov rapidly assembled a planning staff to study the options. He insisted, despite Stalin's insistence on having the results in two days, on first inspecting the terrain for himself. His visit to 57th Army headquarters took place on a clear day. He observed a group of Junkers transports that appeared overhead at about 9,000 feet without a fighter escort. The Russian anti-aircraft batteries grouped in the area opened fire too late; Soviet fighters also arrived too late to intercept. Not a single Junkers had been brought down. Voronov was even more furious when he discovered how little coordination there was between ground observers, anti-aircraft batteries and the fighter squadrons. The major-general in charge of anti-aircraft operations was terrorized into feverish activity.

Back at Zavarykino, Voronov again examined the figures. In spite of the strong German resistance put up early in December, Colonel I. V. Vinogradov, the chief intelligence officer of the Don Front, had not greatly revised his estimate of soldiers trapped in the *Kessel*. He now put them at 86,000, when asked to be precise. It was a figure which was to embarrass Red Army intelligence, especially when their NKVD rivals made sarcastic allusions later.

The draft plan for Operation Ring was at last ready on 27 December, and flown to Moscow. The next day Voronov was told to rewrite it. Stalin insisted that the first phase of the attack, focused on the Karpovka–Marinovka nose in the south-west, should come from the north-west and be coordinated with another operation at the opposite corner of the *Kessel*, cutting off the factory district of Stalingrad and the northern suburbs.

Stalin observed at a meeting of the State Defence Committee that the rivalry between Yeremenko, the commander of the Stalingrad Front, and Rokossovsky, the commander of the Don Front, had to be resolved before Operation Ring began. 'Whom shall we make responsible for the final liquidation of the enemy?' he asked. Somebody mentioned Rokossovsky. Stalin asked Zhukov what he thought.

'Yeremenko will be very hurt', Zhukov observed.

'We are not high-school girls,' Stalin retorted. 'We are Bolsheviks and we must put worthwhile leaders in command.' Zhukov was left to pass on the unwelcome news to Yeremenko.

Rokossovsky, the commander-in-chief responsible for the *coup de grâce* on the Sixth Army, was allowed 47 divisions, 5,610 field guns and heavy mortars and 169 tanks.

This force of 218,000 men was supported by 300 aircraft. But Stalin's impatience again built up, just as he was planning a strike against the Hungarian Second Army. To his fury, he was told that transport difficulties had slowed the delivery of reinforcements, supplies and ammunition. Voronov demanded yet another delay of four days. Stalin's sarcasm was bitter. 'You'll be sitting around there until the Germans take you and Rokossovsky prisoners!' With great reluctance, he agreed to the new date of 10 January.

German officers outside the *Kessel* had been wondering what would happen next. General Fiebig, the commander of VIII Air Corps, wondered after a long conversation with Richthofen: 'Why don't the Russians crush the *Kessel* like a ripe fruit?' Red Army officers on the Don Front were also surprised about the delay, and wondered how long it would be before they received their orders to attack. Voronov, however, had received another call from Moscow now telling him that an ultimatum to the Sixth Army must be prepared.

Voronov, in that first week of January 1943, wrote a draft addressed personally to Paulus. Constant calls from Moscow, with Stalin's amendments, were necessary. When finally approved, it was translated at Don Front headquarters by 'German anti-fascists from the group headed by Walter Ulbricht'. Meanwhile, NKVD representatives and Colonel Vinogradov of Red Army intelligence, displaying their usual rivalry, had begun to search for suitable officers to act as truce envoys. In the end, a compromise was reached. Late in the afternoon of 7 January, Major Aleksandr Mikhailovich Smyslov of army intelligence and Captain Nikolay Dmitrevich Dyatlenko of the NKVD, were selected to go together. Vinogradov, when interviewing Dyatlenko, suddenly asked: 'Are you a *khokhol*?' *Khokhol*, or 'tufty', was the insulting term for a Ukrainian, because Russians were often rude about their traditional style of haircut.

'No, Comrade Colonel,' replied Dyatlenko stiffly. 'I'm a Ukrainian.'

'So you're just like a Russian,' Vinogradov laughed. 'Well done. You are a suitable representative of the Red Army to meet the fascists.'

Smyslov and Dyatlenko were then briefed by General Malinin, the chief-of-staff, and by Voronov himself. One might have thought that Stalin was looking over their shoulder from the way both generals kept asking the envoys whether they fully understood the instructions from Moscow. In fact nobody really had a clear idea of the rules and ritual of a truce envoy. Dyatlenko admitted that his only knowledge came from the play *Field Marshal Kutuzov* by Solovyov.

'So lads,' said Voronov, 'will you fulfil your mission?'

'We will fulfil it, Comrade Colonel-General!' they chanted as one.

Malinin then ordered the front quartermaster-in-chief to kit out the two officers in the smartest uniforms available. The Germans had to be impressed. The quartermaster promised to have them 'dressed like bridegrooms', and winked 'like a magician' at the two envoys. With

Voronov's backing, he had every general's aide at front headquarters on parade in his department. He ordered them all to strip, so that Dyatlenko and Smyslov could try on their uniforms and boots. The two envoys soon found themselves in a Willis staff car, with Colonel Vinogradov. Their destination, they were told, was Kotluban station on 24th Army's sector.

Russian troops in the area had received the order to cease firing from dusk. Then, all through the night, Red Army loudspeakers broadcast a message prepared by Ulbricht's anti-fascists, telling the Germans to expect truce envoys. By the next dawn, 8 January, firing had ceased. Smyslov and Dyatlenko were allotted a tall corporal, equipped with a white flag and a three-note trumpet. 'It was unusually quiet on the snow-covered plain' when they advanced to the very front trenches. The corporal blew the trumpet call: 'Attention! Attention! Everybody listen!' They advanced for about a hundred yards, then firing broke out. The three men were forced to dive for cover behind a low rampart made in the snow by Russian reconnaissance groups for night observation. The 'bridegroom' uniforms soon looked less smart; they also offered little protection from the intense cold.

When the firing died away, Smyslov and Dyatlenko rose to their feet and cautiously recommenced their advance. The corporal also stood up, waving the flag and blowing his trumpet. Once again, the Germans opened fire, but without shooting directly at them. It was clear that they wanted to force the truce envoys to

retreat. After several more attempts, a furious
Vinogradov sent a message forward to call off this
dangerous version of grandmother's footsteps.*

Smyslov and Dyatlenko returned to Front headquarters to report, ashamed at the failure of their
mission. 'Why are your noses hanging down,
Comrades?' asked Voronov. 'The situation is such that
it is not we who should ask them to accept our propos-
als, but vice versa. So we'll give them some more fire,
and they will themselves come begging for them.'
During that night, Russian aircraft flew over German
positions, dropping leaflets printed with the ultimatum
to Paulus, and a message addressed to '*Deutsche Offiziere,
Unteroffiziere und Mannschaften!*', both signed by Voronov
and Rokossovsky. To underline the message, 'they
supported the words with bombs'. Red Army radio
stations also broadcast the text, read by Erich Weinart,
on the frequencies most used by the Germans, and a
number of German wireless operators acknowledged.
The leaflets were certainly read. A captain in the 305th
Infantry Division admitted after capture that officers as
well as soldiers had read the Soviet leaflets in secret,
despite the penalties, 'because forbidden fruit is sweet'.
Sometimes they showed leaflets in Russian to a trusty
Hiwi and asked him to translate. 'Everyone knew about
the ultimatum,' he said.

Smyslov and Dyatlenko had slept for only a couple

---

* Paulus later claimed that he had never issued an order to open fire
on any Russian flag of truce, but Schmidt might well have done.

of hours at front headquarters when they were woken at around midnight. A staff car was outside waiting for them by the time they had dressed in their old uniforms (the ADCs had immediately reclaimed their property). When they reached the intelligence department, they discovered that Colonel Vinogradov had been promoted to Major-General and that they had been awarded the Order of the Red Star. Vinogradov, having joked that he had been promoted 'for all the trousers he had worn out during his service', added that Smyslov and Dyatlenko would receive an even more important medal if they managed to carry out their mission at a second attempt.

The two envoys were told to climb into a staff car with Vinogradov and the officer appointed to replace him as chief of intelligence. As they drove through the night again, the two newly promoted generals sang songs and 'kept interrupting each other with generals' anecdotes'. (Although Dyatlenko's respectful account does not say that they were drunk, they certainly appear to have been celebrating their promotions.) The rhythm of the songs was continually broken, as the staff car lurched in and out of huge potholes along the frozen dirt roads. It was a long journey round the southern side of the *Kessel*, crossing the Don westwards, then back across again at Kalach to the sector covered by the 21st Army. Shortly before dawn, they reached the head-quarters of the 96th Rifle Division, a few miles to the west of Marinovka.

Rather like condemned prisoners, Smyslov and

Dyatlenko were given breakfast, boosted 'by a Narkom's [government minister's] ration'. Vinogradov put a stop to a second helping, and told them to get ready. They then suddenly realized that they had handed the white flag back to the quartermaster at front headquarters. A new one had to be made, using one of the divisional commander's sheets nailed crudely to a branch from an acacia.

The staff car drove them to the front line and parked in a *balka*, from where the party proceeded forwards on foot. Smyslov and Dyatlenko were joined by an elderly warrant officer, with a trumpet, who introduced himself as: 'Commander of the musical platoon Siderov'. A lieutenant also stepped forward and offered to escort them through the minefields – 'because my life is not worth as much as yours,' he explained.

The three envoys put on camouflage suits just behind the front trenches, then set off across the white expanse which blurred into a heavy mist. Some two dozen humps of snow ahead were frozen bodies. General Vinogradov and the other two generals climbed on to a burnt-out Russian tank to watch proceedings. Siderov blew the trumpet. The call 'Attention! Attention!' sounded, in Dyatlenko's ears, more like 'The Last Post'.

As they came closer to the German lines, they saw figures moving. It looked as if the front-line bunkers and trenches were being reinforced. Siderov waved the flag and blew the trumpet again urgently. 'What do you want?' a warrant officer called.

'We are truce envoys from the commander of the

Red Army,' Dyatlenko shouted back in German. 'We are on our way to your commander-in-chief with a message. We ask you to receive us according to international law.'

'Come here then,' he said. Several more heads popped up and guns were levelled at them. Dyatlenko refused to advance until officers were called. Both sides became nervous during the long wait. Eventually, the warrant officer set off towards the rear to fetch his company commander. As soon as he had left, German soldiers stood up and started to banter. '*Rus! Komm, komm!*' they called. One soldier, a short man, bundled in many rags, clambered up on to the parapet of the trench and began to play the fool. He pointed to himself in an operatic parody. '*Ich bin Offizier,*' he sang.

'I can see what sort of an officer you are,' Dyatlenko retorted, and the German soldiers laughed. The joker's companions grabbed his ankles and dragged him back into the trench. Smyslov and Siderov were laughing too.

Finally, the warrant officer returned, accompanied by three officers. The most senior of them asked politely what they wanted. Dyatlenko explained, and asked if they would be received according to international convention, with guarantees for their safety. Complicated discussions followed on detail – whether they should remove their snow suits and have their eyes bandaged – before they were allowed forward. After the officers on both sides had exchanged salutes, Smyslov showed the oilskin packet, addressed to Colonel-General Paulus. The German officers whispered urgently among themselves.

The senior lieutenant then agreed to take the Soviet representatives to their regimental commander. The black blindfolds issued by the front quartermaster the day before had been handed back with the white flag, so they had to improvise with handkerchiefs and belts. All Siderov could offer was the blouse of his snowsuit, and when that was fastened round his head, the German soldiers watching from their bunker entrance burst out laughing. 'Bedouin! Bedouin!' they called.

The senior lieutenant led Dyatlenko by the hand. After a few steps, he asked, 'with a smile in his voice', what was written in the message to Paulus. 'That we should surrender?'

'I am not ordered to know,' Dyatlenko replied, using the formula of the Tsarist army. They changed the subject.

'Tell me please,' said the lieutenant, 'if it is true that a German writer called Willi Bredel has been in Platonovsky? He has been addressing my soldiers on the radio for ten or maybe fourteen days. He appealed to them to surrender, and swore that their lives would be spared. Of course, my soldiers just laughed at him. But was he really here? It was clear from his accent that he was from Hamburg. So was it really him or a record of his voice?'

Dyatlenko longed to reply. Bredel was indeed one of the Germans working for his section and he got on well with him. But if he gave any hint, then the lieutenant would have understood immediately what his 'real job' was. An unplanned diversion occurred at that moment.

The ice on which they were walking was both uneven from shell fire, yet also polished by the passage of boots wrapped in rags. Dyatlenko fell, knocking down the lieutenant. Smyslov, hearing the commotion, shouted in alarm. Dyatlenko reassured Smyslov and apologized to the lieutenant. He was not afraid of a trick. 'About a thousand prisoners of war had passed through my hands by then,' he wrote afterwards. 'I knew their psychology sufficiently well as a result, and I knew that these men would not harm me.'

German soldiers who came to lift the two fallen men slipped over in their turn, making a sprawling mass of bodies. Dyatlenko compared it to the Ukrainian children's game called 'A little heap is too little: someone is needed on top.'

The lieutenant kept up his questioning when the blindfold march resumed, then returned to the question of Bredel. Dyatlenko was less than frank. He said that the name was known to him and he had even read some of his books. Finally, the lieutenant warned him that they were coming to some steps.

The three truce envoys found themselves, when their blindfolds were removed, in a well-built bunker lined with tree-trunks. Dyatlenko noticed two sacks with spoiled grey grain, which they were trying to dry out. 'That serves you right, you snakes,' Dyatlenko thought. 'You burned the Stalingrad grain elevator and now you have to dig food for yourselves out from under the snow.' He also observed the coloured postcards and Christmas paper decorations still in place.

A senior German officer entered and demanded to know the authority for their mission. 'The *Stavka* of the Red Army command,' replied Dyatlenko. The senior officer then left the bunker, presumably to telephone. During the colonel's absence, the German officers and Dyatlenko discussed Christmas celebrations. They then discussed pistols and the Germans admired Dyatlenko's Tokarev. He rapidly surrendered it when the Russian truce envoys realized, to their great embarrassment, that according to international convention they should have left behind their personal weapons.

To maintain the fairly cordial atmosphere, Siderov opened the packet of 'Lux' cigarettes – what Dyatlenko called 'general's cigarettes' – which had been specially issued to them to impress the German officers. 'With great dignity, Siderov offered the packet to the Germans as if he had always smoked the best, and not *makhorka*.' He asked Dyatlenko to tell them that this was his third war: he had fought in 'the Imperialist War, the Civil War and now the Great Patriotic War'. Dyatlenko expected him to add 'against German fascist invaders', but in fact Siderov smiled and said: 'And during all these three wars, I have never had the chance to talk to the enemy so peacefully.' The German officers agreed and added that this little assembly consisted of the most peaceful people on the whole front. Conversation rather came to a halt after that. In the ensuing silence, they heard heavy firing. The Russians were horrified. One of the Germans dashed out of the bunker to discover what was happening. He returned with the accusation: 'It was your people.' Fortunately, the firing soon ceased. (The truce envoys discovered later that it had been Russian anti-aircraft batteries unable to resist the temptation when German transport aircraft appeared overhead.)

Tension rose during the long wait for the colonel's return. But when he came, it was not to announce as expected that a staff car had been sent from Sixth Army headquarters. He had, in Dyatlenko's words, 'a very different expression – like a beaten dog'. The junior officers, guessing what had happened, rose to their feet 'as if a sentence was about to be pronounced on all of them'.

'I am ordered', the colonel announced to the Russians, 'not to take you anywhere, not to accompany you, nor to receive anything from you, only to cover your eyes again, to lead you back, to return your pistols and to guarantee your safety.'

Dyatlenko protested most volubly. He offered, even though it was against his instructions, to give the oilskin packet to a specially authorized officer in return for a receipt.

'I am ordered to take nothing from you,' replied the German colonel.

'Then we ask you to write on the package that you, in accordance with orders received from higher command, refuse to accept the letter addressed to your army commander.' But the colonel refused even to touch the packet. There was nothing left, Smyslov and Dyatlenko concluded, but to allow themselves to be blindfolded again and escorted back. The same senior lieutenant guided Dyatlenko back.

'How old are you?' Dyatlenko whispered after they had set off.

'Twenty-four,' he replied. There were only a few years between them.

'This war between our peoples is a tragic mistake,' Dyatlenko said after a short pause. 'It will finish sooner or later and it would be good for me to meet you on that day, wouldn't it?'

'There is no room for illusions in my heart,' said the German lieutenant, 'because before a month is up, both you and I will be dead.'

'Did you Germans really think', said Dyatlenko, 'that Russia would let you spend a peaceful winter in warm bunkers?'

'No, it was possible to assume from the experience of the past winter that you would launch an offensive. But nobody expected it on such a scale or in such a way.'

'You told me earlier that your soldiers just laugh at the appeals of Willi Bredel.' Out of professional curiosity, Dyatlenko could not resist ignoring his instructions to avoid topical issues. 'But wasn't he right when he spoke about your hopeless situation? Weren't his appeals serious?'

'Everything he said was right,' the lieutenant replied. 'But don't forget one thing. When a war of two world outlooks is going on, it is impossible to persuade enemy soldiers by throwing words across the front lines.'

On reaching the trenches, the eyes of the three Russian officers were uncovered. Their pistols and snow suits were handed back. The two groups of officers faced each other and saluted, then the Russians, under Siderov's flag, returned 'through the white silence' to General Vinogradov who was still waiting by the burnt-out tank.

Vinogradov led them back to the *balka*. The commander of divisional reconnaissance lost no time. 'Siderov,' he said, 'quickly draw me a map of their defences.' The other two truce envoys followed them into a bunker dug into the side of the *balka* and watched 'our old man who spoke to the enemy so peacefully', draw a map of their fire points perfectly. 'I don't know if he had been given this mission from the start,' wrote Dyatlenko afterwards, 'or whether it was just his skill, but it transpired that he had been remembering everything.' Dyatlenko and Symslov then returned to front headquarters in the Willis staff car with the two generals, 'sad and tired' because their mission had been a failure and many men were to die for no purpose.

POCKET PENGUINS

1. Lady Chatterley's Trial
2. **Eric Schlosser** Cogs in the Great Machine
3. **Nick Hornby** Otherwise Pandemonium
4. **Albert Camus** Summer in Algiers
5. **P. D. James** Innocent House
6. **Richard Dawkins** The View from Mount Improbable
7. **India Knight** On Shopping
8. **Marian Keyes** Nothing Bad Ever Happens in Tiffany's
9. **Jorge Luis Borges** The Mirror of Ink
10. **Roald Dahl** A Taste of the Unexpected
11. **Jonathan Safran Foer** The Unabridged Pocketbook of Lightning
12. **Homer** The Cave of the Cyclops
13. **Paul Theroux** Two Stars
14. **Elizabeth David** Of Pageants and Picnics
15. **Anaïs Nin** Artists and Models
16. **Antony Beevor** Christmas at Stalingrad
17. **Gustave Flaubert** The Desert and the Dancing Girls
18. **Anne Frank** The Secret Annexe
19. **James Kelman** Where I Was
20. **Hari Kunzru** Noise
21. **Simon Schama** The Bastille Falls
22. **William Trevor** The Dressmaker's Child
23. **George Orwell** In Defence of English Cooking
24. **Michael Moore** Idiot Nation
25. **Helen Dunmore** Rose, 1944
26. **J. K. Galbraith** The Economics of Innocent Fraud
27. **Gervase Phinn** The School Inspector Calls
28. **W. G. Sebald** Young Austerlitz
29. **Redmond O'Hanlon** Borneo and the Poet
30. **Ali Smith** Ali Smith's Supersonic 70s
31. **Sigmund Freud** Forgetting Things
32. **Simon Armitage** King Arthur in the East Riding
33. **Hunter S. Thompson** Happy Birthday, Jack Nicholson
34. **Vladimir Nabokov** Cloud, Castle, Lake
35. **Niall Ferguson** 1914: Why the World Went to War

POCKET PENGUINS

36. **Muriel Spark** The Snobs
37. **Steven Pinker** Hotheads
38. **Tony Harrison** Under the Clock
39. **John Updike** Three Trips
40. **Will Self** Design Faults in the Volvo 760 Turbo
41. **H. G. Wells** The Country of the Blind
42. **Noam Chomsky** Doctrines and Visions
43. **Jamie Oliver** Something for the Weekend
44. **Virginia Woolf** Street Haunting
45. **Zadie Smith** Martha and Hanwell
46. **John Mortimer** The Scales of Justice
47. **F. Scott Fitzgerald** The Diamond as Big as the Ritz
48. **Roger McGough** The State of Poetry
49. **Ian Kershaw** Death in the Bunker
50. **Gabriel García Márquez** Seventeen Poisoned Englishmen
51. **Steven Runciman** The Assault on Jerusalem
52. **Sue Townsend** The Queen in Hell Close
53. **Primo Levi** Iron Potassium Nickel
54. **Alistair Cooke** Letters from Four Seasons
55. **William Boyd** Protobiography
56. **Robert Graves** Caligula
57. **Melissa Bank** The Worst Thing a Suburban Girl Could Imagine
58. **Truman Capote** My Side of the Matter
59. **David Lodge** Scenes of Academic Life
60. **Anton Chekhov** The Kiss
61. **Claire Tomalin** Young Bysshe
62. **David Cannadine** The Aristocratic Adventurer
63. **P. G. Wodehouse** Jeeves and the Impending Doom
64. **Franz Kafka** The Great Wall of China
65. **Dave Eggers** Short Short Stories
66. **Evelyn Waugh** The Coronation of Haile Selassie
67. **Pat Barker** War Talk
68. **Jonathan Coe** 9th & 13th
69. **John Steinbeck** Murder
70. **Alain de Botton** On Seeing and Noticing